W9-BIZ-274

We Three Kings
and other Christmas Carols

illustrated by

H. A. Rey

Music arranged by Henry F. Waldstein
Music copying and calligraphy by Christina Davidson

HarperFestival®
A Division of HarperCollinsPublishers

O Christmas Tree

German Traditional

2. O Christmas tree, O Christmas tree,
   With happiness we greet you.
   When decked with candles once a year,
   You fill our hearts with Yuletide cheer.
   O Christmas tree, O Christmas tree,
   With happiness we greet you.

O Christmas tree

Good King Wenceslas

Words by J. M. Neale

Moderately

Good King Wen-ces - las looked out On the feast of Steph-en, When the snow lay

round a-bout Deep and crisp and e-ven. Bright-ly shone the moon that night, Though the frost was

cru - el. When a poor man came in sight, Gath'-ring win-ter fu - el.

I Saw Three Ships

English Traditional

2. And what was in those ships all three,
    On Christmas Day, on Christmas Day,
    And what was in those ships all three,
    On Christmas Day in the morning?

3. The Mother fair and Christ were there . . .

4. Pray, whither sailed those ships all three? . . .

5. O, they sailed in to Bethlehem . . .

6. And all the bells on earth shall ring . . .

I saw three ships

I saw three ships come sail-ing in, on Christ-mas day, on Christ-mas day, I

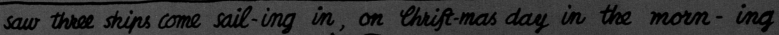

saw three ships come sail-ing in, on Christ-mas day in the morn-ing

Deck the Hall

Welsh Traditional

Merrily

Deck the hall with boughs of hol-ly, Fa-la-la-la-la, la-la-la-la, 'Tis the sea-son to be jol-ly,

Fa-la-la-la-la, la-la-la-la. Don we now our gay ap-par-rel, Fa-la-la, la-la-la,

la-la-la, Troll the an-cient Yule-tide car-ol, Fa-la-la-la-la, la-la-la-la.

2. See the blazing Yule before us,
   Fa-la-la-la-la, la-la-la-la,
   Strike the harp and join the chorus,
   Fa-la-la-la-la, la-la-la-la.
   Follow me in merry measure,
   Fa-la-la, la-la-la, la-la-la,
   While I tell of Yuletide treasure,
   Fa-la-la-la-la, la-la-la-la.

3. Fast away the old year passes,
   Fa-la-la-la-la, la-la-la-la,
   Hail the new, ye lads and lasses,
   Fa-la-la-la-la, la-la-la-la.
   Sing we joyous all together,
   Fa-la-la, la-la-la, la-la-la,
   Heedless of the wind and weather,
   Fa-la-la-la-la, la-la-la-la.

Deck the hall

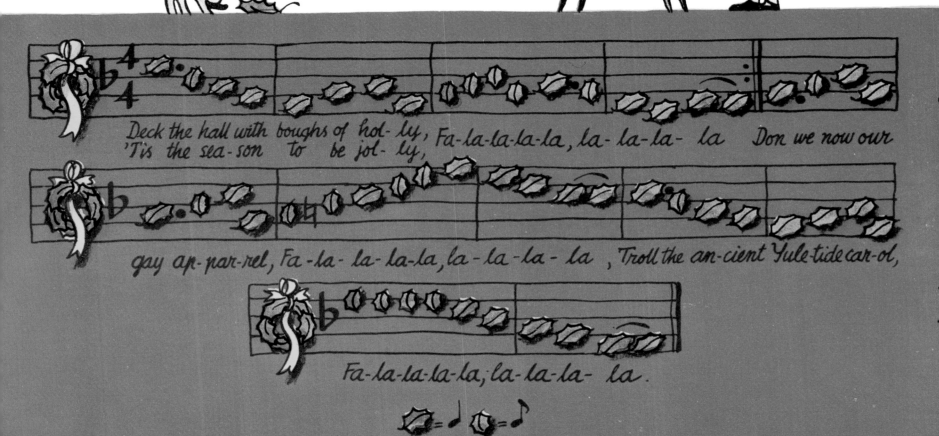

Deck the hall with boughs of hol-ly, Fa-la-la-la-la, la-la-la- la   Don we now our
'Tis the sea-son   to   be jol-ly,

gay ap-par-rel, Fa-la- la- la-la, la-la-la- la , Troll the an-cient Yule-tide car-ol,

Fa-la-la-la-la; la-la-la- la .

O Come, All Ye Faithful

Words and music by J. F. Wade

2. Sing, choirs of angels, sing in exultation,
   Sing all ye citizens of heav'n above.
   Glory to God, glory in the highest.
   Chorus

O come all ye faithful

The First Noel

English Traditional

2. They looked up and saw a star,
   Shining in the East, beyond them far.
   And to the earth it gave great light,
   And so it continued both day and night.
   Chorus

3. This star drew nigh to the Northwest,
   Over Bethlehem it took its rest.
   And there it did both stop and stay,
   Right over the place where Jesus lay.
   Chorus

We Three Kings

Words and music by John Henry Hopkins, Jr.

2. Born a King on Bethlehem's plain,
Gold I bring to crown him again.
King forever, ceasing never,
Over us all to reign.
Chorus

3. Glorious now, behold Him arise,
King and God and Sacrifice,
Alleluia, Alleluia,
Earth to the heav'ns replies.
Chorus

We three kings

We three kings of O- ri -ent are
Bear-ing gifts we trav-erse a- far

field and foun-tain, moor and moun - tain,

fol-low-ing yon-der star. Oh — star of won-der, star of night, star with roy- al

beau-ty bright, West-ward lead-ing still pro-ceed-ing, guide us to the per-fect light.

O Little Town of Bethlehem

Words by Phillips Brooks · Music by Lewis H. Redner

2. For Christ is born of Mary,
And gathered all above,
While mortals sleep, the angels keep
Their watch of wond'ring love.
O morning stars, together
Proclaim the Holy birth!
And praises sing to God the King,
And peace to all on earth.

O little town of Bethlehem

O lit-tle town of Beth-le-hem, How still we see thee lie, A-bove thy deep and dream-less sleep The

si-lent stars go by. Yet in thy dark streets shin-eth the ev-er-lasting light, The hopes and fears of

all the years are met in thee to-night

Hark! the Herald Angels Sing

Words by Charles Wesley · Music by Felix Mendelssohn

2. Mild He lays His glory by,
Born that man no more may die,
Born to raise the sons of earth,
Born to give them second birth.
Risen with healing in His wings,

Light and life to all He brings,
Hail, the Son of Righteousness,
Hail, the heav'n-born Prince of Peace!
Hark! the herald angels sing,
Glory to the newborn King.

Hark! the herald angels sing

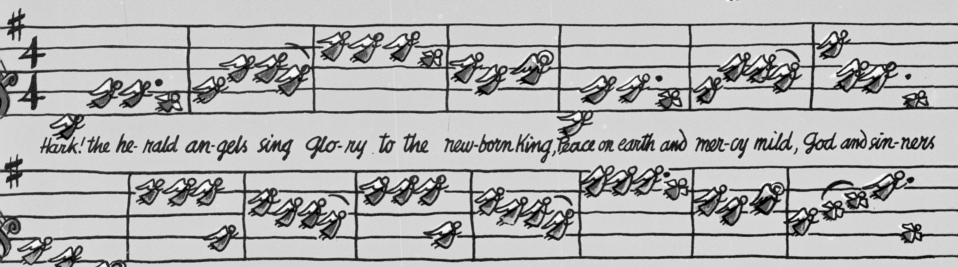

Hark! the he-rald an-gels sing Glo-ry to the new-born King, Peace on earth and mer-cy mild, God and sin-ners

re-con-ciled. Joy-ful all ye na-tions rise, Join the tri-umph of the skies With th'an-gel-ic host pro-claim Christ is born in

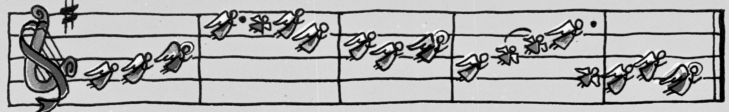

Beth-le-hem, Hark! the he-rald an-gels sing Glo-ry to the new-born King

Silent Night

Words by Joseph Mohr · Music by Franz Gruber

Slowly

Si - lent night, Ho - ly night, All is calm, all is bright.

Round yon Vir - gin Moth - er and Child, Ho - ly In - fant so ten - der and mild,

Sleep in heav - en - ly peace, Sleep in heav - en - ly peace.

2. Silent night, Holy night,
Shepherds quake at the sight.
Glories stream from heaven afar,
Heav'nly hosts sing Alleluia,
Christ the Savior is born!
Christ the Savior is born.

3. Silent night, Holy night,
Son of God, love's pure light.
Radiant beams from Thy Holy face,
With the dawn of redeeming grace,
Jesus, Lord at Thy birth,
Jesus, Lord at Thy birth.